# Up Close

## A CHAPTER BOOK

LOUISE A. GIKOW

## children's press®

**A Division of Scholastic Inc.**

New York   Toronto   London   Auckland   Sydney
Mexico City   New Delhi   Hong Kong
Danbury, Connecticut

For my daughter, who always sees things clearly

ACKNOWLEDGMENTS

The author would like to thank all those who gave their time and knowledge to help with this book. In particular, special thanks go to Dr. Brian J. Ford, Dr. Warnar Moll, Kellar Autumn, Andre Geim, and Dennis Kunkel.

Library of Congress Cataloging-in-Publication Data

Gikow, Louise.
  Up close : a chapter book / by Louise A. Gikow.
     p. cm. – (True tales)
Includes bibliographical references and index.
  ISBN 0-516-23729-2 (lib. bdg.)        0-516-24690-9 (pbk.)
  1. Microscopy–Juvenile literature.
  2. Microscopes–Juvenile literature. I. Title. II. Series.


QH278.G56 2004

                          2004005175

1 2 3 4 5 6 7 8 9 10 R 13 12 11 10 09 08 07 06 05 04

# CONTENTS

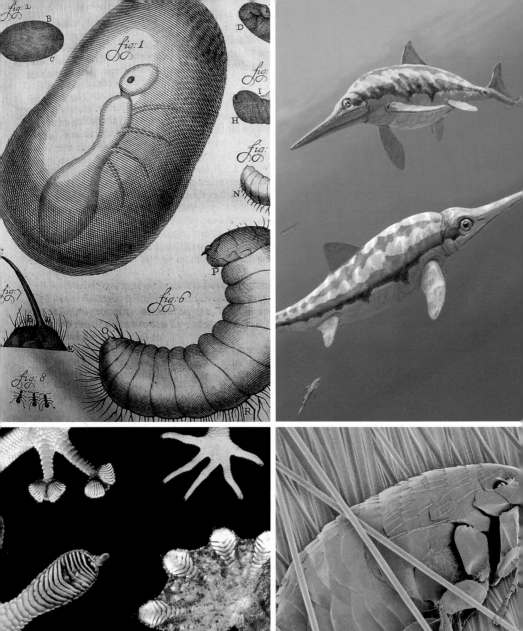

# INTRODUCTION

Microscopes let us look at our world up close. They show us what skin and bone and muscle are made of. They show us a whole world of tiny creatures that are too small to see with our eyes.

In this book, you'll learn about people who use microscopes to study the world around us. Antony van Leeuwenhoek made some of the first microscopes. Looking through one, he discovered tiny animals living in a drop of water. Peter Doyle and Jason Wood used microscopes to study creatures that lived millions of years ago. Kellar Autumn focused his microscope on lizard feet. He wanted to know why certain lizards were able to walk upside-down. Dennis Kunkel used microscopes to find out if life had come back to a lake.

Microscopes are amazing tools. They help us see things that would otherwise remain invisible. Using microscopes, we can better understand our world.

# CHAPTER ONE

# THE MICROSCOPE MAN

Antony van Leeuwenhoek rubbed his eyes. The candle on his desk flickered. It was midnight in Delft, a city in the **Netherlands**. Even though Antony was tired, he couldn't stop working.

In his hand he held a brass metal plate, about the size of a stamp. In it was a small hole with a glass lens. This was one of the first high-powered microscopes in the world.

**Antony van Leeuwenhoek**

This view of the city of Delft was painted in 1661.

Antony became interested in microscopes after visiting friends in London in 1666. While he was there, they showed him a best-selling science book. It was the first popular science book in history. The book was written by an

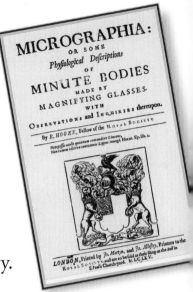

English scientist named Robert Hooke. Inside the book were pages of drawings. They were drawings of the amazing things Hooke had seen through the lenses of his **compound microscope**.

Although the microscope Hooke used was large, not all microscopes had to be so big. One part of Hooke's book showed how people could make a microscope out of a small metal plate and a tiny glass lens. This is what

**Robert Hooke's compound microscope**

Antony decided to do. During the course of his life, he would make more than 500 microscopes.

Antony was born on October 24, 1632, in Delft. His father was a basket maker. His mother came from a family of **brewers**. He went to school until he was sixteen years old. Then he was sent to Amsterdam to become an **apprentice** (uh-PREN-tiss) at a linen draper's shop. He stayed at the shop for six years selling cloth.

Then he went back home to Delft, where he married Barbara de Mey. He bought a house and set up a small business as a linen draper. He and Barbara had five children. All the children, except for one girl, died when they were very young. Maria, the only child who survived, never left home. She helped her father with his work all his life.

After Barbara died in 1666, Antony married again. He stayed in Delft, making microscopes and studying what he found under their lenses.

Antony's microscopes were made from a single lens mounted in a metal plate. The lens didn't move. The object to be

**One of Antony's microscopes**

studied was raised or lowered under the lens using a set of screws. The entire microscope was no more than about 2 inches (5 centimeters) long.

Compound microscopes had already been invented by the time Antony started making

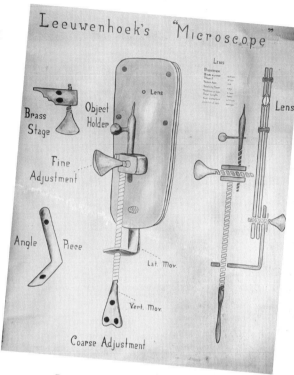

Antony's drawing of a microscope

his microscopes. However, compound microscopes could magnify things only up to about thirty times their natural size. Antony's microscopes could magnify hundreds of times, even though they had only one lens!

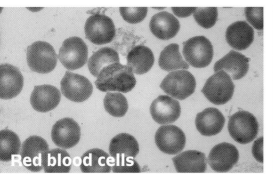

Red blood cells

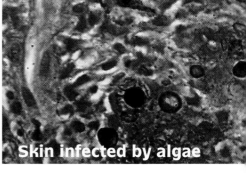

Skin infected by algae

The things that Antony saw with his microscopes were astonishing. He studied pond, lake, and rainwater. In the drops of water he discovered spirogyra (spy-ro-JI-rah) and many kinds of protozoa (pro-toe-ZO-ah). Spirogyra is a type of algae (AL-jee), a plant that grows in the water. Protozoa are tiny one-celled creatures.

Some of these creatures darted about under his microscope. Others slowly oozed along. Some changed shape before Antony's eyes.

Antony examined things that were alive and things that were not. He looked at tissue from animals and plants. He looked at minerals. He looked at fossils.

He even studied his own body, and those of his family and friends. He discovered

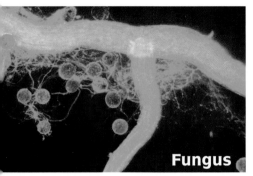
Fungus

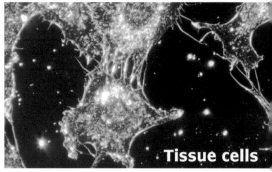
Tissue cells

**bacteria** (bak-TIHR-ee-uh). He found five different kinds of bacteria in his own mouth. He looked at the **plaque** (PLAK) on his teeth. He examined his **feces** (FEE-seez) and discovered special kinds of protozoa and bacteria. He looked at blood and discovered red blood cells. He found that human blood cells were round, while animal blood cells were oval.

He described all of this and much, much more in over 200 letters. He sent these letters to a famous group of scientists in London. They called themselves the Royal Society.

In his letters, Antony described the things he saw in such detail that we can easily recognize them today. He wrote that one kind of protozoa was "fashioned like a bell."

He described the plaque between his teeth as being as thick as batter.

Antony's letters were translated from Dutch and published by the Society. He became famous. In 1680, the Society invited Antony to become a member. It

• was a great honor. It was especially unusual because he never went to London to attend a meeting.

Antony van Leeuwenhoek died on August 26, 1723, at the age of ninety. He never stopped being curious, and he never stopped studying nature through his microscopes.

**Examples from Antony's letters**

**Antony van Leeuwenhoek devoted
fifty years of his life to science.**

# CHAPTER TWO

# JURASSIC VOMIT

The giant **ichthyosaur** (IK-thee-uh-sor) slipped through the **Jurassic** (joo-RA-sik) seas. Strong flippers pushed it through the water. Its long snout moved left and right. Its large eyes scanned the shadowy depths. Fifty feet (15 meters) long and almost 2,000 pounds (907 kilograms), the ichthyosaur was hungry.

A group of shellfish swam nearby. The ichthyosaur opened its mouth, and that was the end of the shellfish, until now.

In February 2002, two British scientists named Peter Doyle and Jason Wood discovered something about the ichthyosaur.

**Peter Doyle**

The scientists were working at the University of Greenwich, in Great Britain. They made their discovery using a microscope.

At the time, they were examining a kind of shellfish under the microscope. The shellfish were a little like squid, but they lived millions of years ago. They are called belemnites (BEH-lem-nites). These belemnites were found in a clay **quarry** (KWOR-ee) in Peterborough, a city north of London. Long ago, the quarry was probably under water. Belemnites must have lived there in great numbers. Ichthyosaurs came to the quarry to eat the belemnites. In turn, the ichthyosaurs were eaten by larger reptiles.

**Belemnites resembled squid (above)**

**A piece of vomit fossil showing the remains of belemnites**

The scientists noticed that the shellfish had some interesting marks on them. It turned out the marks had been made by the acid in **digestive** juices. The juices came from the stomach of an ichthyosaur.

Now, this wasn't surprising. The scientists knew that ichthyosaurs had probably eaten the belemnites. Something about the marks was unusual, however.

The scientists figured out that after the ichthyosaurs ate the belemnites, they threw up, or **regurgitated** (ree-GUR-juh-tate-ed), the belemnites' hard shells.

Why would they do this? The scientists think they know. The ichthyosaurs did it so that the hard shells of the belemnites wouldn't hurt the ichthyosaur's inner organs. In other words, the ichthyosaurs didn't want to get a stomachache!

Today, owls do the same thing when they eat mice. They regurgitate the fur, bones, and teeth. Sperm whales regurgitate the beaks of squid.

**Owls regurgitate pellets. The pellets contain the remains of small animals.**

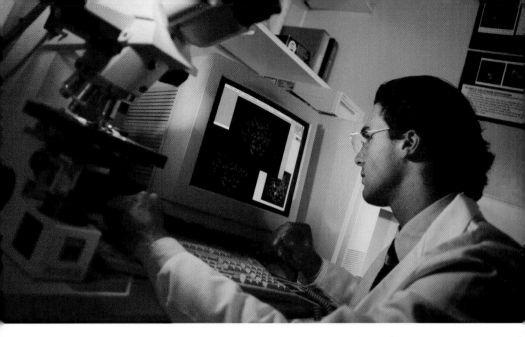

**With a SEM, the magnified object is
seen on a computer screen.**

The microscope that the scientists used
to make this discovery is called a **scanning
electron microscope**. This special microscope,
called SEM for short, was invented in the 1930s.

Before electron microscopes, microscopes
used light to see **specimens**. Using ordinary
light, microscopes can magnify things up to
1,250 times their size. Using special blue light,
they can magnify up to 5,000 times. This isn't
enough to see the tiniest things, however.
For that, a scanning electron microscope
is needed.

Rather than using light, the scanning electron microscope uses **electrons**. Beams of fast-moving electrons are focused on a specimen. The electrons either bounce off the specimen or are absorbed by it. Then a picture is formed on a special photographic plate. Using an electron microscope, scientists can see things as small as an atom, the tiniest particle of matter that exists.

There's only one problem with such a microscope. The electrons in a SEM must be kept in a place that doesn't have air. Living things can't survive in a **vacuum** (VAK-yoom). That means you can't examine anything that's alive using a SEM.

Luckily, the British scientists were studying fossils of shellfish that had lived millions of years ago. For them, the scanning electron microscope was the perfect tool.

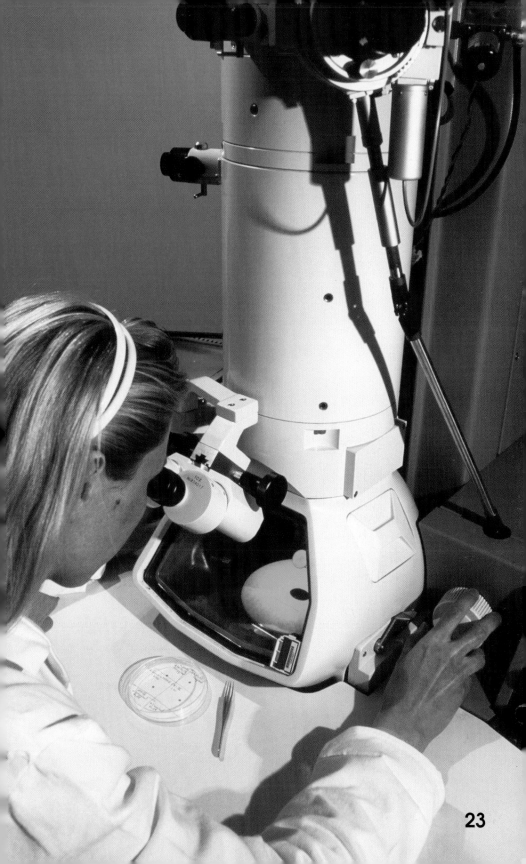

# CHAPTER THREE

# WALKING ON WALLS

In 1997, Kellar Autumn, an American scientist, was on vacation in Hawai'i. One day, while resting in his room, he watched a spider crawl above him. Kellar has a fear of spiders. He tried to get up the courage to catch the spider and put it outside. Suddenly, a **gecko** climbed up to the ceiling. It began walking across the ceiling, upside-down.

**Kellar Autumn studies how geckos climb walls.**

When the gecko saw the spider, it raced over and attacked. The spider fell to the floor, but not the gecko. Kellar wondered how the gecko, a much heavier animal than the spider, managed to stay on the ceiling. What caused its stickiness? For most people, the story would have ended right there. Kellar Autumn is a scientist, however. He has a scientist's curiosity.

**Mediterranean gecko**

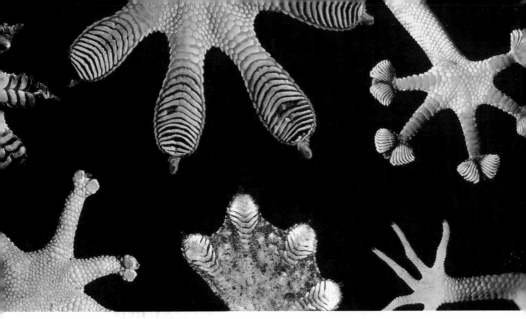

There are 850 kinds of geckos. All have sticky feet.

After his vacation was over, Kellar went back to his lab at Lewis and Clark College in Portland, Oregon. He studied gecko feet under an electron microscope. Geckos' feet are covered with millions of **microscopic** hairs. These hairs are called **setae** (SEE-tee). Each one of these hairs branches off into hundreds of bristles.

Kellar and his team of scientists discovered that the bristles produce weak forces called **van der Waals** (VAN der WOLZ) **forces**. Although these forces work only over short distances, they will stick to almost any surface.

**One hair on a gecko's foot splits into hundreds of bristles.**

The hairs are not sticky by themselves. If they are pressed against a wall, they will fall. They stick only when they are pushed or dragged across a surface. How does a gecko "unstick" itself? The tips of the hairs pop off by increasing the angle at which the hairs touch the surface. According to Kellar, it's as if "geckos have Velcro, but without the other side."

Since geckos have millions of hairs on each foot, the van der Waals forces make their feet very sticky. A gecko can hold up its entire body weight using one toe. If it used all four feet, it could hold up 293 pounds (133 kilograms)!

To show how the van der Waals forces work, Kellar and his team made some tiny foot-hair tips out of two different materials. Both stuck.

Later, a team of scientists at the University of Manchester, England, decided to put Kellar's discovery to use. Andre Geim and his team invented one of the first "gecko tapes."

To create the tape, the scientists made tiny **fibers** out of plastic. The fibers are much shorter than gecko setae and have rounded tips.

Next, the scientists put as many of the fibers that could fit on a tiny square of plastic.

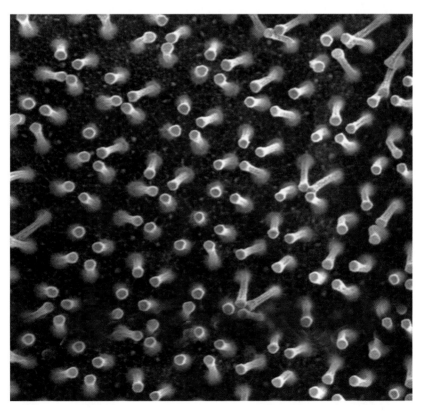

**"Gecko tape" shown under an electron microscope**

Andre and the other scientists wanted to show people how "gecko tape" works. They placed some tape on an action figure's hand. Then they hung the toy from a glass surface. It stayed there for hours.

"Gecko tape" could prove to be even better than tapes that use glue. That's because sooner or later, glue runs out. "Gecko tape" should be able to be reused again and again, as long as it is made out of sturdy enough material. Scientists are working on that now.

"Gecko tape" may be for sale at your local store someday. Then, you could scramble across walls just like a gecko!

**Spiderman hangs from a piece of "gecko tape."**

# CHAPTER FOUR

# TINY LIFE
# IN A BIG LAKE

A helicopter hovered 20 feet (6 meters) above a lake. Its propellers whirred. It was so noisy that Dennis Kunkel couldn't hear the pilot. He could hardly hear himself think.

It was a gray morning in 1990 in the state of Washington. Three months earlier, Mount St. Helens, a nearby volcano, had erupted.

**Dennis Kunkel**

**Mount St. Helens**

The volcano had spewed red-hot lava and ash over miles of mountainside. When Dennis looked down over the burnt earth and dull-gray water, everything seemed dead. Was it really, though?

Dennis wanted to find out. He and other scientists wanted to know how **environments** repair themselves. They wanted to understand how life can start up again after there has been a disaster.

At that moment, Mount St. Helens was a dangerous place to be. The helicopter could

not land. To gather his samples, Dennis had the helicopter door taken off. Slowly, he lowered a bottle attached to a rope into the lake, and he scooped up a sample of water. He had different bottles that could take samples from many different depths. He took some from the surface. He took others from deep in the lake.

Right after the volcano blast, Dennis had looked at samples from the lake. He hadn't seen any signs of life. What would Dennis find this time?

The area around Mount St. Helens after the volcano erupted

Dennis Kunkel came from a small town in Iowa. As a young boy, he was very interested in biology. When he was ten, his parents gave him his first microscope. It magnified things only about 200 to 300 times, but Dennis was fascinated with what he saw under its lenses. He grew up to be a microscopist. A microscopist is a scientist who studies tiny objects with a microscope.

With the help of microscopes, Dennis has learned how muscle cells in a frog's body develop. He had seen how jellyfish

**Dennis collects jellyfish samples from a beach.**

**An ant (left) and strands of spider silk (right) as seen through an electron microscope**

inject poison with their **tentacles** (TEN-tuh-kuhls). He has taken microscopic photographs of these and many other things.

Dennis works with scientists from all over the world. He has helped scientists study pieces of **meteorites** (MEE-tee-ur-rites). He has helped scientists learn more about ants and how they function. He has also used microscopes to study spider silk. This helps scientists find out how it is made and why it is so strong.

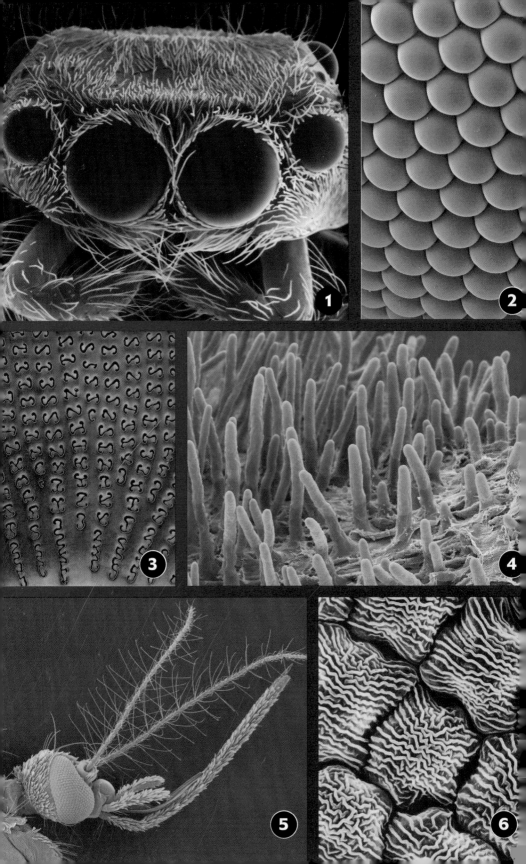

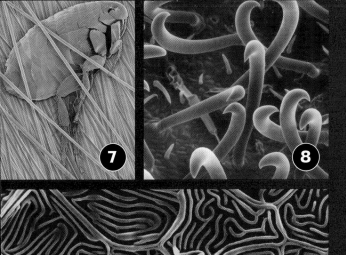

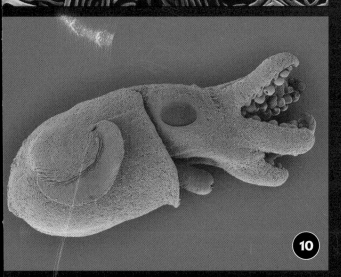

Photos taken by Dennis Kunkel with an electron microscope

1. A jumping spider

2. A mosquito's eye

3. Algae

4. A radish seed

5. A mosquito

6. A mustard plant

7. A flea

8. A seed

9. Goldfish skin

10. A squid

11. Rag weed

39

When Dennis got back from the lake, he started working. In his lab, he made slides of the lake water. Then he put the slides under his microscope and looked at them.

Three months before, there had been nothing alive in the lake. As Dennis focused the lens, he saw some cyanobacteria, a kind of bacteria. These simple life forms told Dennis that life was slowly returning to the area around Mount St. Helens.

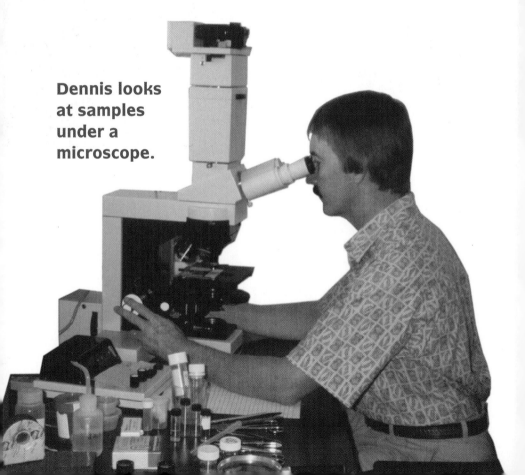

**Dennis looks at samples under a microscope.**

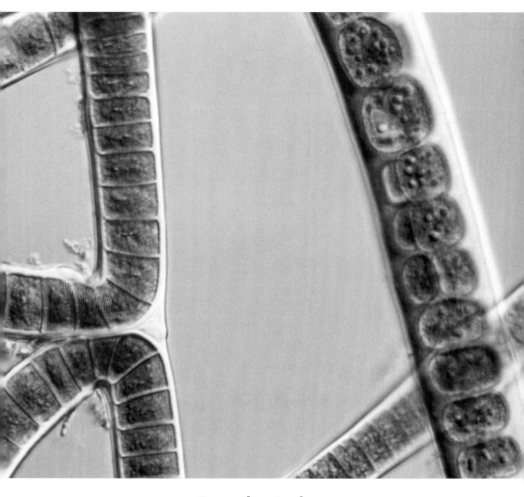

**Cyanobacteria**

A few months later, Dennis found different kinds of algae in the lake. A few months after that, he found even more forms of life in the lake. Soon, simple **invertebrates** (in-VUR-tuh-brits) arrived.

Life traveled to the lake in different ways. Some living things were blown there by the wind. Some swam there through streams that fed the lake. Some simple life forms such as bacteria had probably stayed alive at the very bottom of the lake.

One year after Mount St. Helens erupted, Dennis discovered that fish had returned to the lake. The lake was once more filled with all kinds of life.

"Places like Mount St. Helens can recover from massive natural disasters," Dennis explains. "Will the same fish, the same plants, live again in the lake beneath Mount St. Helens? It is very likely. Simple organisms, such as bacteria and algae, were the first to be re-established in the lakes." Dennis hopes that one day life will again flourish on Mount St. Helens.

Mount St. Helens today

# GLOSSARY

**apprentice** (uh-PREN-tiss) someone who studies a trade under someone already working at it

**bacteria** (bak-TIHR-ee-uh) one-celled animals that are usually harmless, but can sometimes cause illness

**brewer** someone who makes beer

**compound microscope** a microscope that uses more than one lens

**digestive** having to do with the digestive system, the body system that processes food

**electron** a tiny particle that, along with protons and neutrons, makes up atoms

**environment** all the living things and conditions of a place

**feces** (FEE-seez) the waste that comes from your body

**fiber** a long, thin thread of material

**gecko** a small lizard

**ichthyosaur** (IK-thee-uh-sor) a kind of dinosaur that lived in the sea millions of years ago

**invertebrate** (in-VUR-tuh-brit) an animal that does not have a backbone

**Jurassic** (joo-RA-sik) having to do with the time when the dinosaurs lived

**meteorite** (MEE-tee-ur-rite) a rock from outer space that reaches Earth's surface

**microscopic** too small to be seen without a microscope

**Netherlands** a country in northwest Europe

**plaque** (PLAK) a coating made up of bacteria and food that is found on teeth

**quarry** (KWOR-ee) a large hole where something can be mined or dug up

**regurgitate** (ree-GUR-juh-tate) to throw up partly eaten food

**scanning electron microscope** a microscope that uses electrons to make things look up to 300,000 times bigger

**setae** (SEE-tee) hairs too small to see without a microscope

**specimen** something that is looked at under a microscope

**tentacle** (TEN-tuh-kuhl) a long thin growth usually on the head or near the mouths of animals

**vacuum** (VAK-yoom) an area in which there is no air

**van der Waals** (VAN der WOLZ) **forces** weak forces that attract like a magnet

# FIND OUT MORE

### The Microscope Man
www.ucmp.berkeley.edu/history/leeuwenhoek.html
Read more about Antony van Leeuwenhoek and his discoveries with a microscope.

### Jurassic Vomit
http://news.nationalgeographic.com/news/2002/02/0212
_020212_dinovomit.html
Learn more about how scientists discovered the world's oldest vomit.

### Walking on Walls
www.lclark.edu/~autumn/dept/index.html
Dr. Kellar Autumn explains his gecko research on this Web site.

### Tiny Life in a Big Lake
www.denniskunkel.com
See some of the amazing photographs that Dennis Kunkel has taken with electron microscopes.

## More Books to Read

*A World in a Drop of Water: Exploring With a Microscope* by Alvin and Virginia Silverstein, Dover Publications, 1998

*Fun With Your Microscope* by Shar Levine and Leslie Johnstone, Sterling Publishing, 1998

*Hidden Worlds: Looking Through a Scientist's Microscope* by Stephen Kramer, Houghton Mifflin, 2001

# INDEX

# PHOTO CREDITS

# MEET THE AUTHOR

Louise A. Gikow has written hundreds of books, scripts, and songs for kids of all ages (and a few for adults, too). She lives in New York City with her husband, daughter, and two cats. She's worked for Jim Henson Productions and Nickelodeon.

Louise's dad was a doctor, and he had a microscope in his office. When she was young, he used to let her look through it. Later, when she was fifteen, she used it to study fruit flies, which she raised in the basement in little glass jars until they escaped and got into the raisins. She still has the microscope today.